What's in this book

This book belongs to

_____

不一样的季节 Different seasons

学习内容 Contents

沟通 Communication

说说季节
Talk about the seasons

生词 New words

★	冬天	winter
★	夏天	summer
★	已经	already
★	春天	spring
★	秋天	autumn
★	非常	very
★	一点儿	a few, a little
★	云	cloud

啊 (used at the end of the sentence to express appreciation, doubt, urge, etc.)

最近 recently

空调 air conditioner

季节 season

暖和 warm

凉快 cool

冬至
The Winter Solstice Festival

句式 Sentence patterns

我们这里现在是夏天，最近
已经开空调了。
Since it is summer here, we
have already turned on the air-
conditioner.

跨学科学习 Project

介绍一座城市的气候
Introduce the climate of a city

Get ready

1 Which season do you like best?

2 Which season is Christmas in in your country?

3 Which season are Ethan and Ivan in?

"圣诞快乐！现在是冬天，你们为什么不冷啊？"艾文问。

"圣诞快乐！我们这里现在是夏天，最近已经开空调了。"威廉说。

"真有趣！我们的季节不一样啊。春天和秋天呢？"伊森问。

fēi cháng nuǎn huo
非常暖和

liáng kuai
凉快

"春天从九月开始，非常暖和。三月到五月是秋天，很凉快。"米亚说。

有一点儿云
yǒu yī diǎnr yún

"你们那里现在天气真好，天空只有一点儿云，很晴朗。"艾文说。

"快来找我们玩儿吧！过一个不一样的圣诞节。"米亚说。

Let's think

1 Recall the story. When is summer and winter in William and Mia's country? Write the letters.

b 十二月、一月、二月

六月、七月、八月

十二月、一月、二月

Summer

Winter

_____   _____

2 Do you prefer a winter Christmas or a summer Christmas? Discuss with your friend.

夏天比冬天好，
因为我可以……

冬天比夏天好，
因为我喜欢……

10

New words

 1 Learn the new words.

2 Use the words above and the ones you have learnt to talk about the weather today.

1 Listen carefully. Put a tick or a cross.

 2 Look at the pictures. Listen to the story an

1

2

3

4

我是小熊。夏天非常热，天空没有一点儿云，我爱和小鱼去游泳。

冬天，下雪了。天气很冷，我在家里休息。

秋天真凉快。我喜欢和朋友们一起跑跑跳跳。

天气真暖和啊！红的花，绿的草。春天已经来了！

3 Talk about the pictures with your friend.

现在是什么季节？

现在已经是……了，天气……

1

2

3

Task

What is your friends' favourite activity in each of the four seasons? Do a survey and report your results.

活动 \ 季节	春天	夏天	秋天	冬天
打篮球				
踢足球				
跑步				
骑自行车				
游泳				

春天你最喜欢做什么？

春天我最喜欢……

春天喜欢……的人最多。

Game

Listen to the words your teacher says and use them to make sentences.

春天、太阳、暖和、冷。

春天不冷，有太阳，很暖和。

太阳　晴天　暖和　冷　空调

热　凉快　云　下雪　下雨　刮风

春天　夏天　秋天　冬天

Chant

 05 Listen and say.

我有一首四季歌，
请你跟我一起唱。
春天暖和百花笑，
夏天太热开空调，
秋天凉快去郊外，
冬天很冷多睡觉。
春夏秋冬各不同，
四季变化真奇妙。

生活用语 Daily expressions

不用了，谢谢。
No, thanks.

我没事儿。
I am OK.

1 Trace and write the characters.

一 二 三 声 夫 夫 春 春 春

| 春 | 春 | 春 | |

一 二 千 千 禾 禾 秋 秋 秋

| 秋 | 秋 | 秋 | |

ノ ク 久 冬 冬

| 冬 | 冬 | 冬 | |

2 Write and say.

这里___天暖和，___天凉快。

他们非常喜欢___天，因为可以玩雪。

3 Read and circle the correct words.

你喜欢哪个（时间/季节）？
我爸爸喜欢（春天/冬天），他
爱看绿树红花。我妈妈喜欢秋
天，因为秋天很（凉快/热）。
我最喜欢夏天，夏天（一点儿/
非常）热，但是可以吃冰淇淋！

拼音输入法 Pinyin input

Read the paragraph and cross out the two irrelevant sentences. Then type the correct paragraph.

这个女孩是我的朋友。我有五个
好朋友。她是中国人，但是她会说英
语。她的家在上海。北京比上海大。上
海现在是夏天，最近非常热。她喜欢和
她的小狗在花园玩，因为花园里很凉快。

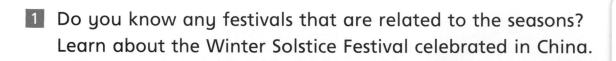
Cultures

1 Do you know any festivals that are related to the seasons? Learn about the Winter Solstice Festival celebrated in China.

今天白天 (day) 最短，夜晚 (night) 最长。

The winter solstice, which occurs on 21, 22 or 23 December, marks the shortest day and the longest night of the year. After that, days get longer and longer.

spring equinox

Sun

summer solstice

winter solstice

autumn equinox

The ancient Chinese celebrated the Winter Solstice Festival (冬至) for the 'return' of the sun. Today it is a day for family reunion. Dumplings and glutinous rice balls are the most popular foods eaten on this day.

2 Australia is in the southern hemisphere. Which date would its winter solstice occur on? Discuss with your friend and circle it.

它的冬天从……月开始，所以……

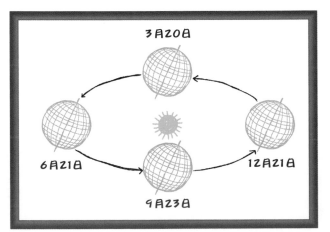

3月20日

6月21日

12月21日

9月23日

Project

1 Did you know that climates vary around the world? Take a look at the climates of some places around the world.

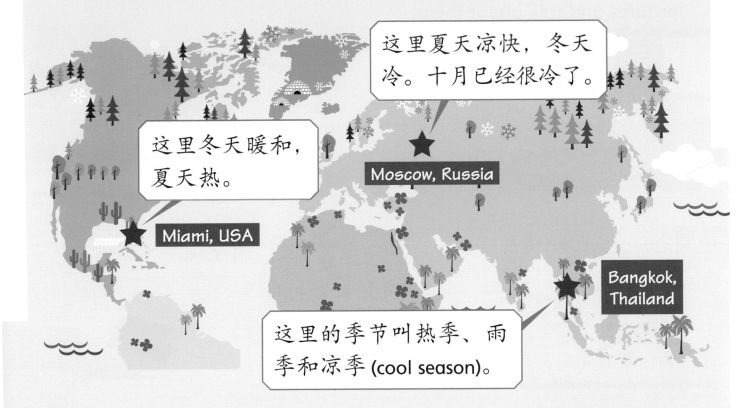

这里夏天凉快，冬天冷。十月已经很冷了。

Moscow, Russia

这里冬天暖和，夏天热。

Miami, USA

Bangkok, Thailand

这里的季节叫热季、雨季和凉季 (cool season)。

2 Paste a photo of your favourite city and introduce it to your friend. Talk about its climate and suggest the best time to visit.

Paste your photo here.

这是……（城市）。

……（季节）是从……月到……月。

……天来这里玩最好，因为天气……

1 The children are decorating the classroom wall with photos of the four seasons. Read the captions and write the characters. Then draw pictures and talk about them.

天

三月

四月

五月

最近有一点儿热。

夏天

已经是夏天了！

六月

七月

有空调，真凉快。

八月

天

天真蓝啊，没有云。

九月

十月

十一月

天

一月

外面非常冷。

二月

十二月

家里很暖和。

2 Work with your friend. Colour the stars and the chillies.

Words	说	读	写
冬天	☆	☆	🌶
夏天	☆	☆	🌶
已经	☆	☆	🌶
春天	☆	☆	🌶
秋天	☆	☆	🌶
非常	☆	☆	🌶
一点儿	☆	☆	🌶
云	☆	☆	🌶
啊	☆	🌶	🌶
最近	☆	🌶	🌶

Words and sentences	说	读	写
空调	☆	🌶	🌶
季节	☆	🌶	🌶
暖和	☆	🌶	🌶
凉快	☆	🌶	🌶
我们这里现在是夏天，最近已经开空调了。	☆	🌶	🌶

Talk about the seasons	☆

3 What does your teacher say?

My teacher says ...

21

分享 Sharing

Words I remember

冬天	dōng tiān	winter
夏天	xià tiān	summer
已经	yǐ jīng	already
春天	chūn tiān	spring
秋天	qiū tiān	autumn
非常	fēi cháng	very
一点儿	yī diǎnr	a few, a little
云	yún	cloud
啊	a	(used at the end of the sentence to express appreciation, doubt, urge, etc.)
最近	zuì jìn	recently
空调	kōng tiáo	air conditioner
季节	jì jié	season

| 暖和 | nuǎn huo | warm |
| 凉快 | liáng kuai | cool |

Other words

圣诞（节）	shèng dàn (jié)	Christmas
有趣	yǒu qù	interesting
一样	yī yàng	same
从	cóng	from
到	dào	to
天空	tiān kōng	sky
只	zhǐ	only
晴朗	qíng lǎng	sunny
快	kuài	quickly
找	zhǎo	to call on
过	guò	to spend

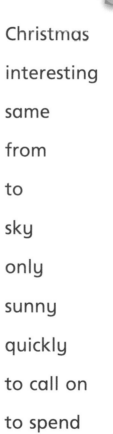

OXFORD
UNIVERSITY PRESS

Oxford University Press is a department of the University of Oxford.
It furthers the University's objective of excellence in research, scholarship,
and education by publishing worldwide. Oxford is a registered trade mark of
Oxford University Press in the UK and in certain other countries

Published in Hong Kong by
Oxford University Press (China) Limited
39th Floor, One Kowloon, 1 Wang Yuen Street, Kowloon Bay,
Hong Kong

Illustrated by Anne Lee, KY Chan and Wildman

Photographs for reproduction permitted by Dreamstime.com

China National Publications Import & Export (Group) Corporation is an authorized distributor of
Oxford Elementary Chinese.

Please contact content@cnpiec.com.cn or 86-10-65856782

ISBN: 978-0-19-047008-1

10 9 8 7 6 5 4 3 2